Tiny House Living

A Complete Guide to Designing and Building a Tiny House

Anthony Hill

Table of Contents

Introduction 1

Chapter 1: Tiny Homes 101 3

Chapter 2: Is This for Me? 13

Chapter 3: Let's Plan 18

Chapter 4: Let's Decorate 33

Chapter 5: Let's Build 47

Conclusion 57

Introduction

The tiny house revolution is quickly taking over the world. A simple internet search of the term "tiny-house" instantaneously generates over 1-billion results! The tiny house revolution is extremely popular all across the globe. It consists of people from all walks of life—couples, singles, nomads, and the elderly. Small spaces have become popular because they are eco-friendly, cost-effective, and provide people with the opportunity to make their dream spaces come to life. Take a moment to think about your favorite spaces growing up and what weird and wacky ideas you had about design. Think about spaces with interesting concepts and unorthodox takes on functionality. Smaller homes are allowing people the opportunity to make these spaces a reality. These homes are a form of creative expression because every home is tailored to the person's needs. Whether you dreamed of staying in a dollhouse, a luxurious mansion, or a man cave where no one would bother you, compact spaces are the solution. The beauty of smaller spaces lies in their ability to fit into everyone's lifestyle. If these spaces have been out of your reach because of the cost, then downsizing is an easy way to make your dream a reality. They allow people the opportunity to take chances with design and think up alternative approaches to roofs and exteriors.

Smaller houses are shaking up ideas around conventional housing. It is liberating people and introducing them to a different way to live. Whether it's an article online or a new TV show on a streaming platform, small-scale houses are a hot topic. Conversations about compact houses are usually met with two reactions: shock steaming from disbelief about how anyone would choose to live this way, or alternatively, complete amazement. The fact that you're reading this book leads me to believe that you form part of the latter group of people who are completely enthralled by the idea of living in a smaller space. There is space for everyone in this community. Small-scale homes are popping up everywhere with more people exploring its possibilities every day. Small-scale home communities are popping up rapidly, with like-minded people choosing to live in the same place. Tiny homes are whatever you choose to make them—whether it's your residence, travel home, or rental property. Smaller meets everyone's needs!

In a community as vast as this, you need a guide that will assist you through every step of making your dream home a reality. Thankfully this is that guide. We will cover every detail of planning and building your tiny home from what materials to use to ensuring functionality. In addition, we will explore the benefits, financial implications, and different types of small-scale houses. Think of this as a guide packed with everything you need to know about going tiny. Let's begin!

Chapter 1: Tiny Homes 101

Firstly, we will answer the most important question: What is a tiny house? There are different opinions on what the requirements are for a space to be considered tiny, but the widely accepted opinion is anything between 60-400 square feet. Small houses date back to the earliest human dwellings. These homes were a necessity for hunter-gatherers as they used them as temporary shelters. Compact spaces evolved from caves, tents, and cottages to what we now know as the modern-day tiny house. We have come a long way from hunting to ensure our existence but the fascination with small spaces has only grown with time. The idea of creating a mobile space provides people with housing security and freedom.

The smallest tiny houses are roughly the size of four treadmills placed side by side. The next time you are at the gym, take a moment to consider living in that amount of space. It might sound like a dream, a welcomed challenge, or nearly impossible. Luckily, there is room for you to pick a space ideal for your needs. You are free to use the standard measurements as a guide for your customized space. Switching from an average-sized traditional home of 2600 square feet or a standard 800 square foot apartment to a smaller space requires research and a shift in your mindset. Downsizing can occur in stages in order to ease you into the transition. Walking through ready-made tiny homes will offer you perspective and allow you to compare the different sizes.

There are two types of small-scale homes: mobile and stationary. Mobile homes are legally classified as recreational vehicles. What sets smaller houses apart from conventional recreational vehicles is their appearance. They are built on trailers and resemble miniature versions of standard houses. The houses are designed to feel homey despite their size. The laws in your state around mobile homes will guide your trailer selection and the size of your home. The maximum measurements for mobile tiny homes are a height of 13.5 feet, a width of 8.5 feet, and a total length of 40 feet. This size allows you to travel with your home without a permit.

Pro tip: Remember when you are designing your home that the total height of your home should be no higher than 13.5 feet when placed on the trailer. This allows you to travel freely without the fear of colliding with bridges.

When you are constructing your home on a trailer you need to think about the weight limit of your towing vehicle. Your home needs to distribute weight equally to be aerodynamic. I suggest avoiding overloading the rear of your trailer to ensure that your home does not scrape the roads when you are traveling over bumps. Mobile houses bring on the additional challenge of deciding where your home will reside the majority of the time. You have the option of parking it in a tiny house community for a monthly fee. This option is perfect for individuals who hope to travel with their homes. You wouldn't be limited by a long-term lease and are free to travel to different cities as you see fit. If you are seeking a long-term option, you can purchase a lot to park your mobile house. This is ideal for individuals who reside in one area for the majority of the year but still want the option to travel with their home. The final option is parking your home in a relative or friend's driveway. This is a cost-effective solution for mobile homeowners.

Small-scale mobile homes come with their advantages and disadvantages. The primary advantage is your ability to travel with your home. There are three disadvantages of mobile homes: depreciation, travel costs, and the precautions that you are required to take when traveling. Your home will depreciate because it is legally considered a vehicle. You should also consider the cost of traveling with your home. You need to budget for increased fuel expenditure and the cost to park your vehicle depending on your preferred option. Your home also needs to be able to endure constant travel; this can cause premature wear and tear. I suggest budgeting for unexpected harm caused to your home if you are constantly traveling. Travelling can also impact the interior of your home. The constant movement shifts your belongings can cause breakage and unexpected damage.

The second type of tiny home is a stationary unit. Simply put, this means that your home is fixed to one location like a traditional home. This type of house is considered an accessory dwelling unit. The law sees it as a smaller space that resides on the same land as a larger building, similar to a garden shed. This allows you to place a compact home in your garden. A stationary compact home has fewer limitations compared to a mobile home because it is not limited by road restrictions. You can build in the parameters of a typical tiny home but you have the opportunity to create a space with more surface area because it is not built on a trailer. Stationary spaces allow you to use stronger materials because you are not limited to weight limits. They are ideal for individuals who want to settle in one place. They are also a great source of income through rental opportunities and sales. Your home becomes an investment because it is not in danger of damage caused by consistent travel, not to mention that your home will require less maintenance. The final advantage of stationary homes is your ability to create a unique space that is not limited by the need to be aerodynamic. Your home can take on any form allowing you to freely express your creativity.

Similar to mobile homes, stationary homes come with their disadvantages. A disadvantage of this method is its location; you need to own the area you are going to build on. The initial cost of the land can be financially draining and will require planning and budgeting. If you are building on land that you already own, this expense is avoidable. This type of ownership becomes an investment, and the compact home can increase the value of your property.

Small-scale homes are constructed from a variety of materials. The materials are dependent on the type of home you want to create. Mobile homes are primarily constructed from wooden framing and trailers. Wooden framing and trailers are durable materials that keep your home within the weight limit. Your small space is also an opportunity for you to create an environmentally friendly building. Many tiny homes are constructed primarily from shipping containers and repurposed wood from older buildings. If you are frugal and willing to repurpose items for other uses you can save money during your build. Stationary homes allow the use of alternative materials such as window walls. You can also construct walls from multiple doors. If you desire a conventional looking home, brick, cement, or wood are ideal options.

Let's Talk About Finances

When you are deciding to become a homeowner, you need to consider the financial implications of your decision. Homes require forethought and extensive planning. If you plan and budget effectively, you can stretch your finances and build your home at the lowest possible price. When you create the budget for your home, you need to start with a list of every item you plan to use in your home. Take this time to plan your dream home, and think big, because there is always an opportunity to cut back later on. Think of every facility that a standard home requires such as electricity, plumbing, and insulation. You need to decide what system you want your home to run on. If your home is mobile, you require an off-grid system. This is initially costly but it saves you money in the end. An off-grid home requires solar paneling and a water system. Your stationary home will either be off-grid or connected to local electrical lines. Your budget should also include furniture costs, monthly expenses, and leeway for unexpected costs.

The beauty of tiny homes is that the size of your home allows you to implement luxurious items at a fraction of the cost. This is great if you are planning to use your home as an opportunity to create your dream space in miniature form. Regardless of your taste, you can achieve a durable home at a fraction of the cost of a traditional home.

If you already own a home and would like to make a lifestyle switch, selling your current home provides you with the funds to start building your small-scale home. This is a big commitment that you thoroughly need to think through but it allows you to dive headfirst into creating your space. If you want to keep your home, you can approach a bank using your home as surety to acquire a loan. Alternatively, you can apply for a personal loan but be mindful of the high-interest rates. Unfortunately, it can be difficult to secure a mortgage for homes this size. The third option for financing a tiny house is simply saving towards your goal. Saving money allows you to avoid the interest rates that banks offer. Moving into a smaller home requires you to drastically downsize and sell your larger furniture and belongings that will no longer fit in your new space, which is a great opportunity to make some extra money to put towards the build!

Once your home is completed, you should ensure its longevity by considering different insurance options. Insuring your stationary compact home requires you to have it certified by the National Organization for Alternative Housing. This increases the likelihood of insuring your home through traditional insurers. Increase your chances further by ensuring that your home meets conventional building standards. If your home does not meet these standards, you will not be paid out when you make a claim. You also need to register your mobile home to qualify for RV insurance. This is a sustainable option if your home is constantly on the move, and also allows you to travel freely with your vehicle without restrictions. Tiny communities have different requirements; some require this insurance in order for your vehicle to park on their premises. I encourage you to consult your insurers during your planning phase as they will assist you with guidelines that you can follow as you build. This ensures that your build meets the insurer's standards.

Self-Build vs. Construction Company

One of the bigger questions that you need to ask yourself early on is whether you are going to construct your home entirely on your own or with the help of a construction company. You have three options: complete self-build, partial self-build, and custom build. A complete self-build means that you will complete the project entirely on your own. This option is easier for individuals who are quick learners or with experience in construction. If you do not consider yourself naturally handy, do not worry, as this book will guide you through the process. You can also learn more about construction through online tutorials and workshops. I suggest practicing your construction skills on a smaller scale project before you build. This gets you accustomed to your tools and gives you the necessary confidence you need to build your home. A benefit of constructing your home is the fulfillment you will experience as you finish every phase of your home. You need motivation and perseverance to build your home. The process will not always go according to plan and you need to prepare for this possibility. Self-builds are popular because they save you money on construction. They allow you to build at your own pace without the added expense of hiring contractors. A disadvantage of a self-build is the space you require to start the project. If you intend on renting a warehouse because you don't own a space large enough for your build or because you reside in an area with unfavorable climate, the rental fee can be costly if your project is extended. This is financially straining if you did not budget for the expense. Despite the uncertainty that comes with a self-build, it can be a great option.

A partial self-build is ideal for individuals who want the fulfillment of building their own home without some of the pressure of constructing it from scratch. A partial self-build means that you will work with a construction company to build various sections of your home. This is usually the frame, roof, insulation, and walls. If you choose this option, I suggest allowing a construction company to work on the larger components of your home. This option gives you peace of mind in the stability of your home. You can be certain that your home's structure is durable, and you will simply be responsible for constructing the interior of your home. If you are a first-time builder, the interior of your home will provide you with enough of a challenge without having to construct the frame. In addition, working with a construction company gives you professional insight into construction. They will assist you in planning your structure and ensure that it is stable. This option is more costly than a self-build but the advantages are clear. You will save time on construction and you are guaranteed a high-quality building. If you prefer to work with individuals, you can compare the cost of purchasing your materials and hiring builders to construct your frame as opposed to working with a company. Alternatively, you can order the pieces you need for your home from a company that specializes in building small-scale homes and assemble them yourself. This takes away the pressure of purchasing materials and calculating dimensions.

A complete custom build is the final option for creating your dream home. This is ideal for individuals who simply want to live in a smaller home as opposed to building one. A custom build is costly as you are purchasing a complete home. Typically, this will be roughly double the cost of a self-build. You can design your home with a reputable company that caters to your needs. A custom home is beneficial because you are guaranteed a home that is correctly built and fully functioning. Your building process follows a strict timeline and you have a clear date for the completion of your home. If a registered professional builds your home, certifying your home as a recreational vehicle or applying for insurance becomes an easier process. This process is stress-free because you can confidently trust your builders. I suggest thoroughly researching different companies and reading customer reviews. This will allow you to make an informed decision and work with a reputable company. It is essential that you openly communicate with your prospective contractor about your expectations and look at previous work they have completed. If your ideas seem unrealistic to them, consider working with other companies.

Chapter 2: Is This for Me?

Tiny homes are extremely popular at the moment, but making the shift is a difficult decision. Traditional homes are considered conventional but smaller homes are quickly becoming the new norm. If you spend your days looking at pictures or watching videos online of compact homes but you still are not sure about making the shift, I will guide you through the benefits of living in a smaller home.

Firstly, we will compare traditional homes with small-scale homes. Are traditional homes that different from small-scale homes? Traditional homes are stationary with a larger surface area, and you can purchase a home through a bank with a mortgage. Traditional homes are of course, widely accepted as the conventional way to live, though that is slowly beginning to change. The purpose of your home differs from person to person depending on your lifestyle. Regardless of whether you seek a secure space for your family, solitude, or room for creative expression, your home should be a space that positively influences you.

On the flip side, a small-scale home offers you the same opportunities as a traditional home. It is tailored to your needs without the large price tag of a traditional home. A smaller home serves as a safe space for your family, a single dwelling, or a space for creative expression. There is no fundamental difference between small-scale and traditional homes, other than their size. Smaller homes are praised for their versatility, because of the changeable nature of the space. If you want to join the tiny community without completely leaving your current lifestyle, you can create an alternative small-scale space. The small amount of space required might even allow you to place it in your garden! You can create a guesthouse, home office, or studio; the possibilities are limited only to your imagination and budget. Furthermore, you can create a mobile smaller space that serves as a traveling home.

A major benefit of living in a smaller home is its ability to shift mindsets around homeownership. We live in a society that is fueled by consumerism and the need for people to purchase goods. People are motivated by their desire to show their wealth through their possessions. This is clear through messaging in the media and the rise in online shopping. It seems like every day there is a new gadget or fashion item launching, and we have become accustomed to this never-ending production cycle. This cycle tricks us into believing that we need to purchase every new item in order not to feel left behind.

Smaller homes are shifting mindsets by allowing people to feel fulfilled by owning less. Your fulfillment will no longer stem from purchasing large items but from living with less. You can feel the same level of fulfillment by owning a smaller home as opposed to a traditional home. Smaller homes allow you to distance yourself from the idea that the more items you purchase the happier and more fulfilled you will be. They enable you to decide what is truly important to you, while simultaneously freeing up money in your budget to pursue those things!

Living in smaller spaces is closely linked to minimalism. Minimal living is a lifestyle that encourages people to live with less. If you limit your items to only the possessions that you need, you will begin to shift your outlook on ownership. The point is not to suffer or live uncomfortably but to understand that your joy does not come from your possessions. If you practice minimalism, you live without the added pressure of excessive ownership. It enables you to live without worry, free from the desire to impress others. Minimalism requires you to be intentional about the items that are in your life. It allows you to be mindful of your environment and conscious of the needs of others.

You can practice minimalism in every area of your life. I suggest beginning by looking at your belongings, room by room. If you identify the purpose of each room, you can then identify what items in that room are a necessity. If you take your bedroom, for example, write down the purpose of the room. Once you have identified the purpose you can keep the items that apply to the purpose. Practice cutting down on unnecessary items by discarding duplicates and unused items.

Fitting in perfectly with the tiny house lifestyle, minimalism is extremely popular with people all across the globe, with millions of people practicing its principles daily. Minimalism allows you to free up your physical space as well as your mental space. If you live in a clutter-free environment, it lowers your stress levels and decreases your risk of mental health issues. A clutter-free space is visually appealing and increases your productivity levels. This is a necessity in a smaller space because you only have limited room to work with. If you live in a small-scale home, you will be forced to minimize your possessions to only those which are essential.

The combination of tiny living and minimalism can lead to financial freedom. These lifestyles come with noticeably lower costs, allowing you to save more money. Smaller homes can also liberate you from borrowing from banks and their steep interest rates. Further, you save money on initial costs such as decorating and designing. Additionally, living in a smaller home limits your number of possessions and stops unnecessary purchasing. The size of your homes saves you money down the line through the upkeep of your home, monthly expenses, electrical, and water bills. Whether you view small-scale homes as a temporary living arrangement or a permanent solution, you can use the time spent living this way to save money.

Similarly, smaller homes are environmentally conscious. We all need to play our part in protecting the environment from further harm. Your home is a large contributor to your carbon footprint, and compact homes are eco-friendly because they utilize less power and produce less waste. If you plan effectively, you can decrease your impact on the environment during construction with the materials you use. Further still, many people choose to power their tiny houses using sustainable energy, which is something you might like to consider!

Living in a smaller home can also give you back your time, as the size of your space saves you time on household chores. This increases your free time and allows you to focus your energy on activities that you actually enjoy! The drastic change of living in a small-scale space can be an opportunity for you to start a new chapter. It's not always an easy task to live completely differently from the way you are accustomed to, but it can be extremely rewarding.

Tiny homes also offer residents the opportunity for a calmer life. In modern times, we are always on the go, rarely allowing ourselves a moment of rest. This is the reality for most of us as we live and work in cities. Downsizing allows you to build a sanctuary for yourself away from the conventional pressures of the world. Reduced living costs might also encourage you to work less, or to take on some more fulfilling but less lucrative work outside of the city.

Chapter 3: Let's Plan

The planning phase of your tiny home is really the most important, as it will save you a lot of time, money, and energy if done thoroughly. Ultimately, you will have to remove quite a few items from the way you currently live and embrace a more minimalistic way of living. Take a moment to consider how you feel about your current house by asking yourself these three questions:

1. What do you hate about your space?
2. What do you love about your space?
3. How would you make your space more efficient?

These questions will allow you to evaluate your habits and how you currently use your space. This will assist you in planning your new space and allow you to tailor it to your specific needs. Once you have identified the most and least used features in your current home, you can decide on what rooms you absolutely need in your new home. An effective way to plan your home is through an activity called "map it out."

- Write down every room you want in your new home on separate pieces of paper.
- Write down the different activities that you want to do in your home.

Match the activity you want to complete with the room where the activity would take place. Try your best to place as many activities as possible in a single room. Once you have compiled your list you can narrow down the number of rooms you need in your home. When you are selecting the size of your home, you can visualize the space by sellotaping out 400 square feet on your floor, or by drawing an outline with chalk. This is 20 feet by 20 feet, and the tape/chalk will help you visualize your space and scale down if necessary.

Once you have mapped out your outline, walk through the space imagining how you would divide the space and what rooms you should include. Outline where you would place your rooms and how you would divide the space. Keep in mind the size of the furniture and appliances you will include in the space. Obviously, the outline doesn't have to be exactly 400 feet. Remember to tailor the size to your specific needs and budget and adjust as you go! This activity will give you perspective and show you the potential of your space. The key to effective planning is research; spend time looking up different furniture companies and customization options. Remember also to research the different energy-saving appliance options as well as space-saving gadgets.

When you are planning your space, you can learn a lot from the homes of other small-scale builders. You can learn from their designs, building methods, and plans. There are numerous tiny home designs out there that you can inspect. It's likely that there are even builders in your local area that specialize in this type of dwelling. If you can't go and inspect other tiny houses in person, then YouTube is a fantastic resource for looking at tiny houses and getting unique design ideas.

Of course, a big decision you'll need to make early on in the planning process is whether you'd like your tiny house to be mobile, or stationary. If you decide on the mobile option, you'll need to begin by choosing a trailer to serve as the foundation.

Selecting a trailer to build your home on is an important decision that requires research. Your trailer should be catered to your needs, and the size of your home is the first aspect you must consider. A flatbed trailer is an ideal choice as it provides you with a smooth area to build your home. Flatbed trailers come in different variations but the important aspects to consider are the tire sizes, brakes, durability, and materials. The trailer needs to carry the weight of your home and withstand constant travel. A brand-new trailer is advisable because you can be certain of its durability. The idea of purchasing a second-hand trailer is tempting because of the price tag, but it can be risky, so keep that in mind. Also, pay attention to your trailer height when making your decisions as it impacts the height of your finished design. There are three primary trailer options for your tiny build:

A Bumper Pull Trailer

This trailer is convenient because of its design and durability. The trailer is easy to travel with and compatible with most towing vehicles. It's also low to the ground, giving you maximum height for your home. This is beneficial especially if you want to create lofts in your home. This trailer type is easy to build on because the wheels do not impact your design, as the wheels are positioned outside of the trailer deck, creating a smooth area to build on.

Gooseneck Trailer

This trailer is ideal for individuals who are building a heavier and larger home. The trailer is easy to tow and distributes the weight of your home effectively. This allows you to travel with your home without worry. Your building process is more complex with this type of trailer because you need to consider the wheels when creating your design.

Custom Trailer

A custom trailer from an accredited company that specializes in building mobile homes provides you with the best choice for your building process. Their trailers are built with your home in mind. You are guaranteed a trailer that is durable, easy to tow, and an ideal size for your build. These trailers typically come with a warranty and are designed to make your build easier.

Additionally, your home's electrical, heating and plumbing system will affect your plan. If your home is off-grid, you require sustainable electrical, heating, and plumbing systems. Solar panels are an easy way to ensure that your home has power and heat. The excess energy that the solar panels catch can be stored in a generator for future use. This ensures that you have power regardless of the weather. The solar panels are effective for your lighting and heating, but I do suggest a propane stove for your cooking, just in case you run out of electricity. Plumbing in your home requires effective planning as it takes up a decent amount of space in your home. There are different water options, as well. You can utilize sustainable water collection systems that work with rainwater. These systems collect rainwater and purify it for your use.

A water tank stored in your home is a convenient way to ensure that your home has a constant source of water. Your water tank can be filled either by rainwater or by a hose. It will require a pressure pump, ventilation system, and a strainer for your water to run smoothly without any impurities. In addition to a freshwater tank, your home requires a black and grey water tank. The black water tank is designated to collect sewage water. The grey tank collects your water waste from the kitchen and bathroom. Discarding this water is a simple task because the water contains limited dirt. If you use organic products, your grey water can be safely discarded in nature. The waste accumulated in your black tank requires special dumping sites. Your waste can be dumped directly into septic tanks, RV communities, water waste treatment plants, and select gas stations. A hose connection, also known as an RV connection, allows you to connect your home through an exterior plug to a water source through a hose. This is a sustainable solution if your home is stationary or located in one place for an extended period. A stationary small-scale home will obviously allow you to make use of existing power grids and plumbing.

Your toilet requires as much research and planning as any other item in your home. You have the option of installing a traditional toilet in your home if your home is stationary. This increases your space because your home no longer requires a grey or black water tank. If your home is not connected to an existing sewer system, you require an alternative solution. An RV toilet is one such alternative solution for your home, and is the closest option to a traditional toilet. The toilet connects to a black tank that collects your waste. This tank requires regular emptying and maintenance with chemicals. Composting toilets are another solution for off-grid homes and environmentally conscious individuals. All you require is a toilet seat, large bucket, plywood, hinges or glue, and sawdust. You can create a functioning composting toilet by following these six steps:

1. Cut out four pieces of plywood that are the height of your bucket. A rectangular structure saves you space and ensures that there is no dead space in your home.

2. Cut out the fifth piece of wood the size of the top of your structure. It will serve as the lid to your toilet.

3. Draw and cut out a hole in the middle of your lid the size of your toilet seat.

4. Using screws and hinges attach your lid to the top of your structure.

5. Place your toilet seat on the top of your structure securing it with screws or glue.

6. Place your bucket in your structure with a cup of sawdust. Your toilet is now completely built and functional.

Remember that every time you use your toilet, you need to place sawdust in the bucket to ensure that your waste decomposes and that smells are reduced. When your toilet is full, you can dump your waste in your composting heap. This is a sustainable solution that saves you space on plumbing. If the idea of emptying your toilet yourself is worrying, installing a self-composting toilet is the ideal solution. Self-composting toilets are costly but they limit odor and require little maintenance. They resemble traditional toilets and are environmentally conscious. The only negative aspect of self-composting toilets is their size. They require ample space for the composting container. If your home is stationary, you can store the container outside of your home. Dry toilets are another option for off-grid homes. They are fairly priced and easy to install. This type of toilet resembles a traditional toilet and runs on an electrical motor. Every time you use the toilet your waste collects into a bag that is stored inside the toilet. The bag is automatically replaced by the motor in preparation for the next time you use the toilet. Once the toilet is full you can easily empty the bags into the garbage. The only work you need to do is to simply replace the bag cartridges and charge the motor. Dry toilets are an ideal solution if you want to live off-grid without having to worry about discarding your waste.

Once you have decided on the size of your space you can create your floor plan. If you have never seen a house's floor plan, I suggest looking up samples on the internet. You do not have to base your drawing on what you see, but it will serve as a guide to assist you in creating your space. When you are creating your floor plan, decide first on the scale of your drawing. Start with a blank sheet of paper and create the shape of your home. Once you have your shape in place, indicate the thickness of your walls. Your drawing will now resemble a thin border of your home. Indicate where you want to place your windows, doors, and walls. Draw in all of your fixed items like your shower, toilet, and built-in cabinets. When you are creating your plan, consider your current lifestyle and your future goals. The foundation of your home can be built on concrete, wood, or a trailer for mobility. Keep in mind maintaining equal weight distribution when you are building your home on a trailer. This ensures that your home is aerodynamic and is not weighted down on a single end.

Alternatively, you can create your layout digitally by using software. These computer programs allow you to type in the dimensions of your home and assist you in dividing up your space. You can easily make changes to your drawings on these programs. Some programs also allow you to select furniture and create an accurate 3D image of your home.

If you are using a professional company to create your design, you will have the option to make adjustments to their existing templates. Many builders will be happy to work with you in customizing a plan that fits your specific vision.

The design of your roof needs to account for all weather conditions. An effective roof design protects your home from water damage and strong wind conditions. When you are designing your roof, you need to consider its shape and purpose. Your roof design needs to allow water to easily fall off it without collecting in one area. A slightly angled roof is ideal for modern and futuristic designs. It reduces the height of your home and saves you money on material costs. An angled roof prevents any water build-up and protects your homes and belongings. A traditional roof is ideal for a stationary home because you are not limited by height requirements. These roofs allow water to easily flow off them as they are shaped like prisms.

Once you have completed your floor plan you can create a timeline for your build. You need to decide on the materials that you will use and where you will acquire them. Sourcing your materials requires research and effective planning. Sourcing materials is easier if you are using conventional materials that you can source from your local hardware store. A standard compact home requires the following materials:

- Wood of your choice for the frame of the home
- Plywood
- Insulation in the form of styrofoam and house wrap
- Windows
- A door and hardware

- Roofing of your choice
- Flooring

These basic materials allow you to build the shell of your home. Depending on the scale of your build, your materials may require a few weeks to be delivered. Take this into account when you are creating your building schedule. If you are using recycled material, you need to account for the time it requires to source your material. When you are ordering your material, it's wise to order a few extras items of each material to account for breakage or losses.

The space you use to build is extremely important during your planning stage. If you do not have a space of your own that will accommodate the size of your home during the build, then you will need to research a space to rent. Warehouses or construction companies often offer people the opportunity to utilize their space at a monthly rental fee.

When you create your building plan, account for the assistance you will require. Are you going to ask your friends and family to assist you occasionally to lift materials or are you going to hire builders on specific days? If you are receiving free assistance from your friends and family, ensure that you plan effectively to suit their schedules. If you do not have past building experience, allocate time for mistakes and learning. If you intend to hire builders or tradesmen to assist you, plan efficiently to ensure that you hire them for the correct amount of time. This should be a manageable expense because of the size of your home. Experienced builders and tradesmen can work quickly and efficiently to complete specific tasks in a short amount of time.

If you are a first-time builder, your tool supplies are likely limited. We will explore renting equipment versus purchasing equipment. You can save on your budget by renting specific tools that you do not require every day. This helps you save money on purchasing the items and space for storage. Rental stores simplify your building process by delivering and collecting the necessary tools. If you require large tools for just a few hours, rental is an ideal option. Renting equipment requires you to follow a strict building schedule. When you have the tools, ensure that you complete all of your preparation work. This means that if you are using a large saw to cut your framing, cut all of your pieces at the very beginning of your build. This makes assembly easier and limits the amount of time you need to rent your tools. When you are renting equipment, ensure that you check these three aspects:

- Check that the tool is functioning correctly.
- Rent the tool with the instruction manuals.
- Ask for a tutorial on how to use the tool to ensure that you use it safely and correctly.

Renting a tool comes with the possibility of accidental damage and theft that you will need to cover. Discuss this with your rental store to understand the potential fees and budget for this expense. You can often save money on your rental fees by comparing the daily rate on different days. If you rent your equipment over a weekend, it will typically be cheaper! Purchase items that you will use frequently and intend to use after your build is completed. Items like a drill, screwdriver, hammer, pliers, handsaw, wrench, artisan level, and safety equipment are recommended purchases. You will use them daily and the cost to rent will eventually add up to the cost to purchase.

Room Plans

When you are planning your home, it is helpful to understand the process you will take for each space. If you create a plan for each room, you will be able to work with a schedule that allows you to effectively manage your time. Your building plan should follow a weekly schedule with set targets for your build. Prior to the building process, you need to apply for the building permits that allow you to add an extension to your existing home or start a completely new project. This is dependent on the local laws in your areas and building codes. If you plan to apply for insurance, ensure that you apply for the necessary paperwork and follow their building guidelines before you begin.

The following is a sample schedule to give you an idea of how you might like to plan your build:

Week One: This is the first week of your construction project. You need to ensure that all your materials have been delivered and are in the correct quantity. If your build requires a building permit, ensure that you have received your permit and legal documentation. Once you have checked your materials, clean your building site and the area you want to construct. If you are building on a trailer, ensure that it is in place and ready for construction.

Week Two: This is when your construction begins. Plan to lay your foundation followed by erecting your home's frame, roof, and side paneling. Inspect your framing and ensure it is up to code and safe. Remember to protect your frame from bad weather with a protective covering.

Week Three: Install your plumbing, electrical lines, insulation, drywall, windows, skylight, and doors. This week completes the shell of your home as it begins to take form.

Week Four: Plan to paint your home's interior and exterior. Install your light features and electrical plugs.

Week Five: Install your flooring, tiling, built-in cabinetry, and bathroom features.

Week Six: Complete your home's exterior features such as lighting, cladding, and trims.

The exterior of your home is based on your preferences, but you have the option to create a home that suits your environment. Your home can resemble its surroundings—for example, you can create a log cabin or an eco-friendly home built from reclaimed wood in the forest. This allows your home to blend into your surroundings without negatively affecting the environment. If your home is in your backyard, you can create a miniature version of your home or a minimal structure to blend into the surroundings. Think of this during your planning and designing phase of your project. Tiny homes can also serve as an opportunity for you to build unconventional structures and designs. You can use your home as an opportunity to make a statement!

Chapter 4: Let's Decorate

Once you have planned your home, some of your architectural decisions will impact your home's design. Your home is not limited by the exterior; it is an opportunity to display your taste and design preferences. In a smaller home, every space is important; as such, you need to be intentional about your design decisions. I will start by taking you through the different external design styles for your home. There are 10 main design styles listed below that will assist you in identifying your preferences.

1. **Victorian**-style homes are easy to identify because of their distinct features. The homes reflect the popular features of homes in the Victorian era. The homes are identified through their steep roofs, gables at the front of the home, and bay windows. You can modernize Victorian homes by using bright colors on traditional features.

2. **Colonial** homes feature asymmetrical designs in the home's shape and features. The homes are rectangular or square. They have distinct windows with shutters, and the homes are made of brick or wood. They reflect European homes during the colonial era; the homes look formal.

3. **Farm**-style homes are growing in popularity as they offer a comfortable homey feel. The homes focus on functionality and simplicity. They are easily identifiable by their wooden exterior and large porches. The homes are typically white with large windows. A cost-effective solution for achieving this look is through reclaimed wood and quality paint.

4. **Cottage**-style homes are the easiest to duplicate in small-scale homes because of their size. Cottage-style homes are wooden, brick, or built with a log exterior. The homes usually have chimneys and are characterized by their warm inviting exterior. Achieving this look in your home is possible through using reclaimed wood and logs.

5. **Industrial** homes are modern and symmetrical. They use metals, concrete, and brick. The homes mirror buildings from the industrial era like factories and warehouses. The homes are often cold because of the rough metals. The style is considered masculine and modern. You can of course, combine one style with another for a softer look. In smaller homes, you can incorporate this style by using shipping containers, metal sheets, and steel-framed windows. If the home is stationary, concrete is an alternative material that is cost-effective and easy to maintain.

6. **Bohemian** homes are identified by their free-flowing style and use of combined textures. This style uses different colors and encourages people to try different things. You can include this in the exterior of your home by using different paint colors, woods, and lighting. Combine similar shades of complementary colors for a relaxed and inviting exterior.

7. **Modern** homes have clear lines and shapes. They use a mixture of materials such as glass, concrete, and metal. Implementing these modern elements to your home design requires the use of clear shapes and neutral colors. An easy way to implement modern aspects in your home design is through steel lighting, dark roofing, and steel windows.

8. **Contemporary** design goes hand in hand with modern design. The primary difference is the use of relaxed lines and shapes. The style implements curves and creates a warm atmosphere with cold material. Implementing tech accessories in your home's exterior is an easy way to create a contemporary look.

9. **Futuristic** design is a style catered to out-of-the-box thinkers. The design pushes the boundaries on convention by using unexpected shapes, colors, and

materials. Implement futuristic design in your tiny home through conceptual design—for example, give your home a theme.

10. **Minimalist** design is increasingly popular with the rise of minimalism. We have already discussed the basic principles of minimalism, and minimal design follows a similar principle. You live with less and decorate with less. The principle follows simplicity and neutral colors. Implementing minimalism into your exterior requires straight lines and simple designs. Keep your exterior as simple as possible without clutter and distractions. The aim is to create a design that celebrates space.

Understanding Color

The exterior of your home will influence the design that you carry through into your home. The colors you choose are vital to the overall look of your home. You need to be mindful of your color choices and their impact on your overall design. Here, I will take you through the different color options for your home's interior and exterior. The colors you choose are based on your preferences, but specific colors are appropriate for certain styles. The colors are divided into three main categories. Primary colors serve as the base of the wheel, which are: red, blue, and yellow. They are followed by secondary colors purple, green, and orange. These colors are created by combining primary colors. The final category is tertiary colors created by combining secondary and primary colors. The six color groupings are based on the sequence on a color wheel. The colors follow the following sequence: Yellow, yellow-orange, orange, orange-red, red, red-purple, purple, purple-blue, blue, blue-green, green, green-yellow.

There are six types of color groupings that you can implement in your home:

1. The first is **monochromatic**. This color grouping requires you to use one color throughout your home in different shades. For your home's exterior, implement a monochromatic style by using different shades of a single color on your roof, door, window trims, and wall. This creates a seamless result as the colors blend well with one another. A monochromatic color scheme can create a calming or dramatic effect depending on the colors you choose.

2. You can implement an **analogous** color scheme. These are colors that appear next to one another on a standard color wheel. The colors complement one another because

they have similar tones. You can combine purple, purple-blue, and blue because the middle shade is a combination of the two colors. This combination for your home's exterior creates an eye-catching and confident design.

3. **Complementary** color groupings utilize colors that lay directly opposite one another on the color wheel. The colors create a drastic contrast that makes your home eye-catching and creates a bold look. This combination creates a dramatic contrast and a positive space because of the brightness of the colors.

4. **Triadic** grouping is three colors that have an equal amount of space between them on the color wheel. These are colors that lay with three colors in between them on a color wheel. The colors create a bright colorful environment.

5. **Split-complementary** colors use a combination of four colors on the wheel. It uses two colors that lay directly next to one another and the two colors that lay directly opposite them. This combination creates eye-catching moments on your exterior. I suggest leaving space between the different colors to create different focal points in your design.

6. **Double complementary** colors are two sets of colors that lay directly opposite one another. In order to identify these colors, select one set of complementary colors as your base. If you leave a single space from your base you can identify your second set of complementary colors. When you look at the color wheel, the two sets of complementary colors should create a rectangle. I suggest using these colors in four different tones. This makes the colors easier to use and less strenuous on your eyes. If you enjoy using bright colors, implement them through your accessories. You can implement this grouping on the exterior of your home through your windows, door, and roof. A bright door is an effective way to include color in your home.

Room by Room

The color principles also apply to the interior of your home. When you are deciding on the design style for the interior of your home, the colors you choose alter the space. I will guide you through designing your home's spaces room by room. We will explore different layouts, luxury vs. cost-effective items, color, and multi-purpose furniture.

The kitchen is described as the heart of the home. Regardless of whether you are a gourmet chef or an amateur chef, a kitchen is a necessity in a home. Your kitchen requires five basic components: A fridge, stove, counter space, sink, and cabinets. These five components make up a basic kitchen. The positioning of your kitchen will influence the size of your cabinets and countertops. If you place your kitchen at the end of your home in an L shape, it creates a larger surface area for your cabinets and countertops. Placing your kitchen in the middle of your home against one wall allows you to manage your limited area by creating an open-plan environment. This layout allows you to create a designated kitchen area in your home without closing off the space. You can use the area opposite your kitchen to serve as a continuation of your living room. If you prefer a smaller kitchen, place it against the width of your room. This type of design is efficient and allows you to create specific sections in your home.

The size of your kitchen is also dependent on the number of appliances you plan on installing. If you want to incorporate a dishwasher and washing machine into your space take this into consideration when you are planning. An effective way to store your dishwasher and laundry machine is in a vertical cabinet. This saves you space as you place the machines on top of one another.

In your kitchen, the question of luxury vs. cost-effective is dependent on your taste, but I suggest investing in quality appliances. This saves you money over time and saves you energy. A cost-effective method for building a kitchen is to create your countertops from wood or concrete. This is ideal for modern, futuristic, industrial, minimalistic, and farm-style homes. Stones like granite and marble are ideal for Victorian, colonial, and minimalistic homes. Stone counter spaces are easy to clean and make homes feel luxurious.

The color of your kitchen influences the appearance of its size. White creates the illusion of a bigger space and increases the light in the room. A monochromatic approach to your kitchen is another great way to make the space feel larger. Incorporate multi-purpose storage options in your kitchen through sliding cabinets and dividers. This helps you utilize narrow spaces effectively.

Pro tip: Organize your kitchen utensils and pots with hanging hooks. This saves you cabinet space and allows you to use the vertical space in your home.

The bathroom in your home should be inviting and feel luxurious. A bathroom is a space that can create a statement in your home. The layout of your bathroom is dependent on the items you want to include in your space. You need a toilet, sink, shower, or bathtub. A bathtub in a compact home is possible with a custom-cut tub. A shower is the expected option in a smaller home as it utilizes less space, or you can opt for a 2-in-1 tub and shower.

The placement of your bathroom in your home is effective under the loft space or across the width of a back wall. This allows you to create an asymmetrical space without dividing your living area. If you prefer to utilize the length of your home, design your bathroom below your loft, if you have one. You can divide the space under your loft into two sections creating two separate spaces.

Implementing luxurious items in your bathroom is cost-effective because of the size of the space. You can use high-quality tiles, finishes, and materials. The type of tile you use will connect your bathroom design with the other spaces in your home. Lighter colors and mirrors create an open space and assist in adding dimension. Mirrors and glass showers create the illusion that the room is larger than it actually is. You can also create a functional space in your bathroom by utilizing floating shelves as opposed to bathroom cabinets.

Pro tip: Use a leaning ladder by your toilet to create an effective storage area for your towels, products, or decorative pieces.

Your living room is the common area in your home. It serves as a spot to entertain guests, relax, and as a spare bedroom. Your living room is the largest room in your home and will likely be where you first enter. The design of your living room needs to create an easy flow and increase functionality. There are two potential places for your living room—in the middle of or at the end of your home. If your living area is in the middle of your home, you can create an open space that connects to your kitchen. This creates an open-plan area to socialize. Your living room requires a sofa, or chairs and a table. You can include optional items like a television in the space. A space-saving living room in the middle of your home can be made with a sleeper couch and a retractable table. Multipurpose furniture in your living room allows you to create extra storage opportunities in your home.

If your living room is at the end of your home, consider building a raised sofa. A built-in sofa allows you to create storage space under your sofa in the form of drawers or hidden slots under your cushions. A raised living area adds dimension and helps create separate rooms in an open-plan space. If you prefer store-bought furniture, purchase an L-shaped sofa that fills the width of your space. When you are selecting a sofa, select a durable fabric like linen, cotton, or leather.

A space-saving technique is mounting your television to a wall or placing it behind a piece of artwork. You can save money by decorating your space with furniture from thrift stores or by upcycling your current furniture. It's a good idea for tables in smaller homes to be multifunctional and removable. If you have a fixed table, it limits your floor space. Foldable tables are popular in these homes because they can easily be stored away. Alternatively, you can create a custom foldable table that is mounted to your wall. This solution is advantageous for people who utilize tables frequently for their meals or work. Your living room may be small, but your design choice can increase its perceived size through your use of color and light.

Bedrooms in tiny homes are usually found in lofts or a designated space on the first floor. Loft bedrooms are popular in small-scale homes because they allow you to utilize the height of your home. Building a loft allows you to create an extra room that does not affect the square footage of your home. Loft bedrooms are ideal for individuals who are not afraid of small spaces. The room can feel cramped so you need to ensure that there is ample light and windows. You can create your loft lower down in your home, allowing the space to be bigger. This increases the head room in your loft, reducing any anxiousness associated with small spaces. You can fit two lofts in your home, creating a spare bedroom or extra area. When you are decorating your bedroom, keep in mind that it is an area that needs high-quality items. This is essential especially in a loft because you want to create a calming space that is conducive to sleep. Invest in a high-quality mattress and bedding. This creates a comfortable and calming area. If you create a bedroom on the first level of your home, you can place it in a pullout compartment under your built-in sofa or create a multifunctional space that will serve as your bedroom. I suggest utilizing a corner of your home if your living area is in the middle of your home. If your bedroom is multifunctional, you can use a foldable bed to save space during the day. This allows you to use your bedroom for your other needs during the day. Get the most out of your room by using hanging lights and floating shelves as opposed to using side tables. Create extra storage in your space for your clothing by utilizing a standing rail or pull-out drawers under your bed. Alternatively, you can use a loft as your wardrobe.

A space-saving hack is using your staircase as a storage opportunity. If you use traditional stairs in your home, they are less strenuous on your back and are multi-functional. You can place a cut-out in your staircase to display your interests. The nook can be used to store your shoes, books, music, or artwork. It will serve a functional purpose and also decorate your space. If you do not want your items constantly on display, you can make your staircase multifunctional by installing a door. The door will allow you to easily access the area while storing away any items you do not want on display.

You can also use a loft to store your seasonal clothing, blankets, or extra essentials. Extra shelving across the length of your roof can create more storage opportunities that blend in with your home. An unexpected storage area that is ideal for a compact home is under your floor. In a traditional home, you would typically have a basement or attic to store seasonal items. You can implement this into your home by creating storage boxes under your floor.

I believe that every small-scale home should have a special space based on your interest or hobbies. This personalizes your home and allows you to get the most out of it. You have the opportunity to create any space that suits your interests from a reading corner, office, art room, or sewing corner. If you planned effectively, your space can be built into your floor or fold down from your ceiling. Designating space in your home requires creativity and efficient design. If you want to create a home office, install a wall-mounted fold-down desk that you can easily store away. A reading corner requires a comfortable seat or cushions; all you require is a few throw pillows and a blanket to create it. You need to be willing to think outside of the box to find different ways to use your existing spaces in your home. The design allows you to make your rooms multi-functional while remaining practical.

Chapter 5: Let's Build

Once you have completed your planning and designing stage, the next step is to build your home. This may seem daunting, but if you follow your plan you should not run into any construction issues. I will guide you through the different stages of building your home from laying your foundation to nailing your final piece of cladding. The instructions are dependent on the type of build you are completing (complete self-build or partial self-build) but are beneficial for both models.

Preparation

Examine your building site, leveling off the ground and ensuring that the area is clean. If you are building a stationary home, ensure that you mark off your construction site with tape to indicate your working area. If you are building a mobile home, ensure that your trailer is clean and that the rear support jacks are attached firmly to the ground. Purchase a trailer that has the rear support jacks already attached as opposed to purchasing them separately.

Foundation

The foundation of your home is the starting point of your build. You have three foundation options: You can pour a concrete foundation that covers the surface area of your marked building location. A concrete foundation requires you to dig 3 inches into the ground and pour a standard concrete mix. A pillar foundation is built on four standard concrete pillars that you can purchase from your local hardware store. Set the pillars in the four corners of your home, ensuring that they are firmly placed in the ground. You will build your flooring on top of this frame. Building a foundation on a trailer requires you to lay pillars next to one another across the length of your trailer. Secure these pillars in place with a staple gun or with nails. Secure your pillars to your trailer using bolts to secure them in place.

Flooring

Creating your flooring requires you to lay pillars in the shape of your home's outline, securing them together with nails. Remember to check that your structure is leveled before moving onto your next step. Once you have created your outline, secure it to your foundation using nails. In order to strengthen the surface, cut out and place pillars the width of your structure in your outline. Select the number of pillars you would like to use and establish their placement by dividing the number of pillars by the size of your frame. Do not fill the entire frame, leave space between the pillars that you will fill with insulation. I suggest placing ten pillars in the outline with an even amount of space between each one. Cut and place your foam insulation to fit into the empty spaces in your floor's outline. Lastly, create the top layer of your flooring by securing plywood to the outline you have created.

Building Your Frame

Build your frame as a single piece that you will secure to your finished flooring with anchors. The easiest way to build a frame is by cutting out your pillars to their desired lengths, similar to the outline you created for your flooring. Your wall frame follows the same process. Start by assembling the outline of your frame, ensuring that it is the desired length and height of your walls. Mark where the openings of your windows and door will be. Create your frame around these openings by filling the space with pillars. Place the pillars at an equal distance from one another along the length of your frame. Once you have secured your long pillars, strengthen your structure with pillars cut to the correct size that fit the width of your structure. Your completed frame should be a single piece with openings for your windows and door. Follow this process for all the walls in your home. Alternatively, you can build your framing out of metal.

Completing Exterior Walls

Once you have erected your frames and attached them firmly to one another using anchors and screws, you can begin sheeting your walls. Using a hand drill or staple gun, attach plywood to the exterior of your home. Cut the plywood to size to ensure that it frames your windows and doors.

Roofing

Depending on the roof design you have selected, your roof will require angled wood as the base. The angles you create will be the trusses of your roof. Start by cutting the wood to your desired size and secure the wood to your home with nails. Once you have created your trusses by joining two pieces of wood, cut at a right angle and attach sheathing in the form of plywood to your frame. To ensure that your roof is protected from water damage, attach eave flashing to the border, securing it with staples. The final step is to attach your metal sheeting to the top of your roof using roofing screws followed by your gables.

Weatherproof Your Home

Wrap your home in house wrap to protect it from moisture damage. You can purchase house wrap in large rolls. Install it by rolling it onto the sides of your home and attaching it with staples. Secure it with sealant tape to ensure that it is firmly attached to your home.

Install Windows, Doors, and Skylights

The windows and doors in your home require accuracy to ensure that they are correctly installed. Do not be afraid to reinstall your windows until they are correctly leveled and sealed. When you are installing your windows, place them in your window's openings to ensure that they fit correctly. Seal your windows in place with a window sealant of your choice. Install your door frame and door using hinges, ensuring that they fit without any gapping. If you are struggling to install your windows and doors correctly, consider hiring a professional to assist you in the process. Finish the exterior of your home with crack fillers and sealants for any gaps.

Plumbing and Electricity

Your home's plumbing and electrical connections are dependent on the system you have selected for your home. The plumbing of your home requires professional installation to ensure that it is functioning correctly. This ensures that you do not experience unwanted water damage or connection issues. Incorrect plumbing also leads to water waste. Additionally, you need to install your water tanks at this time if your home is off-grid. Your power cables need to be installed at this stage in your build if you are using an alternative power source like solar panels to ensure that they are secured to your home and connected to the correct wiring. This installation requires a professional to ensure that it is safely completed and functioning correctly.

Interior Insulation

Insulate the interior of your home by cutting foam insulation to size and placing it in your walls. Secure your foam by spraying the perimeters with spray foam to eliminate any gaps in your insulation. Once you have completed your insulation installation, complete your wall by sheathing with plywood or drywall. Secure your sheathing in place with screws.

Flooring and Trim

Your home's flooring is vital to the overall look. Wooden flooring is durable and easy to maintain. It creates a warm, homey atmosphere as opposed to tiling. I suggest wooden flooring for your small-scale space as it is cost-effective compared to installing hardwood in a standard-sized home because of the amount of space you need to cover. Install your flooring by laying out the individual pieces one at a time and simply slotting them into one another. Floor installations are easy to complete and hassle-free. Insert all of your trims around your flooring and plugs to create a finished look.

Paint

Once your walls have been completely sheathed, begin to paint your home with a base layer of primer. This ensures that your selected paint color matches the color in the container. If you are unsure of your color choice, paint a small section of your wall and allow it to dry. This allows you to test out your color before committing it to your entire space. Remember to protect your flooring from any paint spill and tape off your windows and door frames. Once you have painted your home, you can remove the tape to reveal seamless paint edges.

Install Cabinets and Interior Items

The next step in your building process is installing the interior cabinets and appliances. Tackle each space one at a time to ensure that you are not overwhelmed by the work that needs to be completed. I suggest starting with your bathroom. Once your plumbing has been connected, you can install your shower and the corresponding tiling. When you are installing your tiling, ensure that it is correctly leveled and grouted into place. The shape of your tile impacts the difficulty level of installation. If you are a first-time tiler, opt for a geometrical design with straight edges. Install your chosen toilet and cabinet to complete the room.

Tackle your kitchen by installing your cabinets and attach your appliances to your power source. Once these are securely in place, install your kitchen sink and countertop. If your countertop is marble or stone, consider hiring a professional to install it. This prevents damage, as the stone can be extremely fragile. Alternatively, use durable wood for your countertop.

Exterior Paint and Cladding

The final step in completing your home is finishing your exterior. Once you have decided on your finish, you can complete your home. Wooden cladding is a durable option that provides you with a finished look. Attach the cladding to your home with staples, starting from the base of your home and working your way up. Layer your cladding one on top of the other as you work up your exterior walls. Once you have completed this step, proceed to paint your cladding with durable paint specifically for wooden cladding. This ensures that the finished product dries correctly and ages well over the years. You can also opt for a simple paint to complete your home as opposed to cladding. This will give your home a minimal look. I suggest painting your home a contrasting color to your window frames. This ensures that your home looks complete regardless of the style.

Safety

When you are living in a smaller home you need to put safety measures in place to ensure that your home is secure at all times. You want to prevent people from stealing or damaging your home. If you have a mobile home, you require a hitch lock and wheel block. A hitch lock attaches to your trailer's hitch preventing it from attaching to a vehicle. This prevents anyone from towing your vehicle without your permission. A wheel block locks onto your trailer wheels locking them in place. It adds a level of security to your trailer and ensures that your home is fixed in its desired place.

Standard locks installed on the inside of your windows and doors are an affordable security solution that prevents anyone from entering your home. Additionally, security cameras and motion sensors allow you to monitor your home from a remote location. You can connect your security cameras with a mobile application that allows you to monitor your home from your phone. These systems send notifications to your phone if there is any movement around your home or if your doors open. If you live in a tiny home community, you have the added security of other homes around you.

The internal security of your home is as important as the external. Your space will need smoke detectors, fire extinguishers, and possibly air purifiers. The small size of the space can make it easy for moisture to build up and accumulate in your walls. The buildup of air can also make your home seem cramped and congested. Clean your air with an exhaust fan to ensure your health and the health of your home. A simple fix to filter your space is making use of your windows. Open your windows regularly and allow fresh air to flow through your space. This cleans your space and saves you money by limiting your use of air conditioning systems. If you remain mindful of your needs as well as the needs of your home, you can easily protect your space from unwanted damage.

Conclusion

Building a home is not an overnight process, but if you have learned anything from this book, I hope that it is confidence in what is possible. I hope that this guide has opened your mind to new ways to live. We have covered everything from picking a trailer and insurance, to color theory and decorating. Whether you are a recent graduate or are newly retired, there is a place for you in the tiny community. Small-scale homes offer you a unique opportunity to own a fully functional home at a fraction of the traditional cost. This added financial freedom allows you to use your money on what matters to you most, as opposed to on mortgages and bank loans. Once you rid yourself of the financial burden of a traditional home you can shift your lifestyle, choose to work less or save towards your other goals. Money will no longer be a stressor in your day-to-day life.

Smaller homes are an opportunity for versatility and multifunctional spaces. They are travel homes, rental properties, residences, home offices, guesthouses, or studios. Compact homes are limited only by your imagination and are driven by your needs. Whether you intend to stay in a small-scale home for the rest of your life or it is a transitional home, small homes can accommodate every stage of life.

Small-scale living is an adventure regardless of your surroundings. It offers you the opportunity to live with the daily necessities we are accustomed to, just on a smaller scale. You will likely learn that you can live with less and are happier doing so.

Sustainable living is a concept that we should all aim to implement in our lives. Compact homes help you lower your carbon footprint and limit your home's effect on the earth. They allow you to remain environmentally conscious, thanks to their size. You will use less power and create less waste. You also have the option of living off-grid, ensuring that your energy is from a sustainable source, like solar panels, as opposed to fossil fuels.

Living tiny does not equate to discomfort—it can mean luxury, durability, and creative uses of space. The size of your home can allow you to include high-quality items at a fraction of the cost.

Remember that every small home is not the same, so choose items that make sense for you. Simple decisions like your paint color, toilet type, and faucets make a world of difference. Planning is key to ensure that you produce a space you truly love. Every square foot of your home is important!

Welcome to the tiny revolution.

www.ingramcontent.com/pod-product-compliance
Lightning Source LLC
LaVergne TN
LVHW021737060526
838200LV00052B/3318